Alon
The Otter

Chips Barber

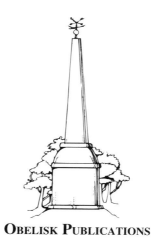

OBELISK PUBLICATIONS

ALSO BY THE AUTHOR

The Lost City of Exeter / The Great Little Exeter Book
The Ghosts of Exeter / Beautiful Exeter
Topsham Past and Present
Around & About the Haldon Hills–Revisited
Diary of a Dartmoor Walker / Diary of a Devonshire Walker
The Great Little Dartmoor Book / The Great Little Totnes Book
Made in Devon / Burgh Island and Bigbury Bay
Dark & Dastardly Dartmoor / Weird and Wonderful Dartmoor
Tales of the Teign / The Great Little Chagford Book
Ten Family Walks on Dartmoor / Ten Family Walks in East Devon
Six Short Pub Walks on Dartmoor
The Great Little Plymouth Book / Plymouth in Colour
Ghastly and Ghostly Devon / Dawlish and Dawlish Warren
The South Hams / Beautiful Dartmoor
Torquay / Paignton / Brixham
Around & About Salcombe / Around & About Seaton and Beer
Around & About Sidmouth / Around & About Teignmouth and Shaldon
From the Dart to the Start / Dartmouth and Kingswear
Cranmere Pool – the First Dartmoor Letterbox
Haunted Pubs in Devon
Brixham of Yesteryear Parts I, II and III
Teign Valley of Yesteryear Parts I and II
Princetown of Yesteryear Parts I and II
Pinhoe of Yesteryear Parts I and II
Torbay in Colour–Torquay, Paignton, Brixham
Widecombe–A Visitor's Guide
Newton Ferrers & Noss Mayo

We have over 140 Devon titles; for further details please send SAE to
Obelisk Publications, 2 Church Hill, Pinhoe, Exeter, EX4 9ER, or tel (01392) 468556

Acknowledgments

Thanks to the staff of the West Country Studies Library in Exeter,
Heather Gilling and Len Bastyan
All pictures by or belonging to Chips Barber apart from:
Ron Lumber, pages 10 (bottom), 16 (top), 18, 20 (top), 22, 28
Ann Elford, page 13 (top)
Helen Bamber, page 16 (bottom)
Kath Kingdon, page 17
Map on page 32 redrawn from an out-of-copyright source by Sally Barber

First published in 1996 by
Obelisk Publications, 2 Church Hill, Pinhoe, Exeter, Devon
Designed and Typeset by Sally Barber
Printed in Great Britain by
The Devonshire Press Limited, Torquay, Devon

Along The Otter

Local people will tell you that the River Otter has two 'heads' – where the river rises is Otter Head and where it falls into the sea is also Otter Head. This book is a journey between these two heads ...

The Upper Reaches

The River Otter rises, as a trickle, high in the Blackdown Hills, at a point on the slope of North Down. For about two miles it flows through Somerset before tinkling over the county boundary into its real homeland of Devon. But there aren't many to witness this homecoming for this is quiet country, a high plateau of over 800 feet above sea level, where the villages are well spread and our 'river' is nothing more than an infant flow. This high plateau is cut up by numerous streams that carve deep depressions in the landscape as they radiate off the flat-topped watershed of the Blackdowns. The Culm, which gives its name to Culmstock, Uffculme, and Cullompton, rises just a short distance away to the north west of the Otter's source. The Yarty rises just on the other side of the Brown Down ridge, one followed by the B3170, a road that crosses the Blackdowns before dropping down to Taunton and an altogether more urban world. Other streams that rise a little to the north are tributaries of the River Tone and their waters eventually pour into the Bristol Channel. Therefore the Blackdowns are the true divide, or watershed, of this region.

These uplands make good walking country and there are plenty of footpaths but you will not find many ramblers to make it seem crowded, unlike parts of distant Dartmoor, which can be glimpsed from some vantage points in the Blackdown Hills.

In its first mile the Otter trickles through fields passing close to Otterford's lovely church, alone apart from a few cottages. Almost immediately the youthful Otter drops steeply down to fill the Otterhead Lakes, a delightful spot for some fly fishing although, if truth be told, I think the fishermen would rather catch fish than flies! The path between the higher and middle lakes with its flint stones is hard on the feet so, if you walk there, make sure that you have plenty of tread on your footwear! But this attractive country is definitely best seen and appreciated on foot.

The Otter is essentially a river with a sunny disposition for it heads southwards towards the sun for long parts of its course. It flows on in its valley beneath the high, compact, almost forgotten, village of Churchinford, a place that is so close to Devon, and so far into the corner of the county, that it has been omitted from several guide books to Somerset!

From Upottery to Honiton

As the river gains momentum several small tributary streams add to its flow, each coming down its own short valley. The scenery around the upper Otter valley is typical Blackdowns countryside, expansive flattish hilltops, punctuated by deep, steep combes. The Otter is not stalked by any major road in these parts so makes its way in pleasant peacefulness. The first place of any size that the Otter encounters, in Devon, is the small village of Upottery, which sits snugly in the deep valley but on a low divide above the Otter.

David Young, the well-known West Country television presenter, lived here with his wife, Labrador dog, Oliver, and their cats for several years before moving to Sidmouth. He would have been well aware of the connection between this village and his later home, hinted at in the village pub's name, the Sidmouth Arms.

A succession of events, spanning a number of years, led to this Sidmouth connection. The Manor was purchased in 1759 by Dr Anthony Addington, who was the physician to the Tory Prime Minister, Lord Chatham (1766–68). The doctor's son, Henry, was involved in politics, rising to become Speaker of the House of Commons in 1789. He was an ambitious man who went on to succeed William Pitt as Prime Minister in 1801. He held this premier post for three years, acquiring the title of Viscount Sidmouth. In his later years he held the post of Home Secretary, spending as much time as his career would allow at his home in Upottery, until his death in 1844.

The village vicar from 1886 to 1923 was the Rev. John Jane. His sons delighted in playing with their boats on a pond in the corner of the vicarage meadow. Here they re-enacted many a famous sea battle; who would have thought that one of them would one day become an expert on such matters? Thus it was that 'Jane's Fighting Ships' was

'born' as the result of a childhood spent by a pond in Upottery.

Until the early 1950s the village had its own fire brigade, which kept its hand pump in a cottage located between the war memorial and the church. These days the 600 or so residents of the parish have to wait, in times of crisis, for the fire engine to get to them from farther afield.

There have been many changes in the village since those days when there was a cattle fair (and also an annual ploughing match) held each 17 October. In the mid-nineteenth century it was a much livelier place, *White's Directory for Devon* listing two pubs, the Devonshire Inn and the George Inn. There was also a shoemaker, wheelwrights, a corn miller, a tailor, a mason, two shops, a post office and a blacksmith. The war memorial now stands on the site where the village blacksmith used to ply his trade. No longer does the postman do his rounds on horseback as he did until 1954. He had the equine perk that gave him a horse to use on the weekend hunts. On retirement the horse was put out to graze in the Manor park running down to the Otter. The present Manor House was built for Viscount Sidmouth in about 1845 but has seen other uses. Early in the First World War Belgian troops arrived at the house, part of which was used as a convalescent home. As they couldn't go home they were later transferred to one of Lord Sidmouth's cottages at nearby Rawridge, a little way down the Otter valley. Their place was then taken by British troops.

Mohun is an ancient name in Devon and has links with many places. If you look at a map of this part of the Otter valley you will see 'Mohun's Ottery', on the hill above the river farther along the valley towards Honiton. A branch of one of Devon's most famous families, the Carews, lived here. Sir William Carew had a gifted, but somewhat indolent, son Peter, whom he sent to school in Exeter. But the sixteenth-century lad was a restless soul who preferred to spend his time dodging school to enjoy sports and amusements of various types. When his father found out about his son's wanderings he was furious with him. Carew Senior had to do something drastic so, with no time to lose, he hastened to Exeter. Peter must have been taken aback when his father pulled a dog collar from his pocket, then placed it around his son's neck before leading him all the way back to Mohun's Ottery.

Sir William had heard of a new school in London that might just sort his son out and duly packed him off. But still there was no joy for Sir William as his son just didn't want to know about anything academic. Peter, too, was suffering from his father's great expectations. He befriended an influential, well-connected Frenchman who took him to France. The upshot of this was that Peter was given a military grounding, taking to it like the proverbial duck to water. Although young he impressed many powerful people and, with his new-found skills, soon came his own riches of both the material and the social type. He even impressed Henry VIII!

Thus it was at the still tender age of eighteen, years after he had left his native Otter valley abode in the hills, the once-reluctant pupil, prodigal Peter, came home. He was now much taller, beautifully attired and on a splendid steed. He rode into the courtyard at Mohun's Ottery. His family did not recognise him as he knelt before them to ask for their blessing; they were totally bemused – why should an apparent stranger crave such an indulgence from them? Slowly the penny dropped as to who the 'stranger in their midst' was and they were overjoyed to discover that their misfit of a son had turned into such a fine, accomplished young man. Thus this became a story with a happy ending as he had been offered a place at the court of Henry VIII. Sir Peter Carew (1512–1575) probably rebuilt Mohun's Ottery as his initials appear in the spandrels of the doorway.

The River Otter wends its way through its steep-sided valley, for the most part between typical East Devon plateaus but there are some striking exceptions, most notably Dumpdon Hill. This is one of the most distinct landmarks in the area and if there is a uniformity in the landscape, when viewed from a distance, this unusual tree-topped hill projects out into the valley as something out of the ordinary. There is public access to the top and an information board tells all – but I will leave that one for you to discover for yourself!

Another significant tributary of the Otter runs down the deep depression just to the west of Dumpdon Hill. It is a small river system in its own right with several small clear streams, all rising in the vicinity of Luppitt, and combining to eventually discharge, as one, into the Otter at Langford Bridge.

Just across the valley from Dumpdon Hill is Monkton, a small village with some fine buildings. However the majority of people, who speedily pass through on the ever-busy A30, hardly give them a second glance. This is a dangerous stretch of road where there have, sadly, been a number of fatal accidents in recent years.

Combe Raleigh, about a mile to the north of Honiton, is a small village of about 200 people. If awards were made for stability in population, then this little place would be a strong candidate. In 1931 it had 188 residents. Thirty years later it had 187 and in the two following census returns it stayed at that same figure! No doubt this was a case of older ones passing on to be replaced by the newly-born or newcomers but a graph to show these demographics would show a line on an amazingly even keel. No other place along the Otter could say the same. Compared to Monkton's traffic flow, Combe Raleigh is quiet by contrast. It has some fine buildings that include its church and its ancient chantry house, situated beside a small tributary of the Otter. The village was owned by the Raleighs in the thirteenth century and, as we will see later, not the only one along the Otter to include this name. The Combe part of the place name means 'in a valley' so when you see this little village snugly tucked away from the rigours of the prevailing winds, you will know that its name makes sense.

In a book of this nature it's not possible to do full justice to the larger places along the banks of the Otter so here are just a few, almost random details about one of Devon's most historic towns.

Honiton

Honiton has one of the longest, straightest and widest main streets, for a town of its size, in England. People old enough to remember the days before the Honiton bypass, which runs parallel to the River Otter for several miles, will recall just how long it took to travel from one end of the town to the other on summer Saturdays in the past. Being on the main London to Exeter road the town has never been a stranger to traffic passing through and, at some 16 miles from Exeter, for many years reaped the financial benefits from stage coach travellers and the trade they generated.

Honiton has had various industries – the woollen trade flourished in the seventeenth and eighteenth centuries, but it is most famous for its lace and its pottery. At one time the manufacture of serges employed over a thousand of the townsfolk but the local industry declined when industries polarised and developed in the North of England. As a market centre Honiton served a wide area and it was common to see that wide main street filled with farm animals.

Before the arrival of the railways market towns, like Honiton, were far more important because it was difficult and impractical for people on foot to travel any great distance for shopping or trading. Therefore there would be a market town almost every eight to ten miles across the country, and they would have been real centres of activity, of hustle and bustle and of great importance to the catchment areas that they serviced. Honiton had its own privileges and developed its own customs out of importance as a market town. In July each year the Town Crier, sporting his cocked hat and his braided cloak, carries a long pole through the streets. Atop the pole is a glove garlanded in flowers, which is displayed at one of the pubs in the town. He cries out, three times, "Oyez, the Glove is up, the Fair has begun. No man shall be arrested until the Glove is taken down. God Save the Queen."

The ceremony that follows is mentioned in Arthur Mee's *Devon*, first published in 1938: "Then from the window of an inn handfuls of hot pennies are thrown into the street and children burn their fingers with them and cool them in the stream which is conveniently running for them by the kerb." This little runnel was called The Lakes. A nearby holy well was noted, not for healing burnt fingers, but for curing eye disorders.

Some people who were arrested, outside the days of the Fair, were punished and humiliated in a most public manner at Honiton. John Rice and Robert Pile indulged in 'scrumping' for apples and were publicly whipped. The last lady to be treated to a short, damp ride on the ducking stool, in 1770, was dunked because she was discovered, in the cellar of a house, sleeping off the effects of an almighty drinking binge. I bet she sobered up quite quickly!

Some nineteenth-century Honiton hoodlums committed a much more serious crime at Colyton. They waited for the vicar to leave the church and then stole all the church silver. Thinking that they had got clean away, without detection, they returned to Honiton in triumph. They decided to celebrate and stashed the stolen goods underneath the settle in an alehouse. Unbeknown to them, a stout and upright Colytonian had witnessed their suspicious exit and, on discovering the nature of the crime, went in hot pursuit making enquiries as he went. His trail took him across East Devon to Honiton where his detective

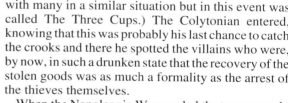

instincts told him that the baddies would probably be found in a pub. Of course, Honiton's long main street is almost a mile in length, and in those long ago days it had many pubs, cider houses and inns, being on the main coaching route from Exeter to London.

The resolute Colytonian, unfortunately for him, chose to enter the town from the east and one by one systematically searched each pub. His enquiries took him from inn to inn until he entered the very last one, on the western edge of the town, several hours after having searched the first on the eastern side. (The pub should have been called The First and Last in keeping with many in a similar situation but in this event was called The Three Cups.) The Colytonian entered, knowing that this was probably his last chance to catch the crooks and there he spotted the villains who were, by now, in such a drunken state that the recovery of the stolen goods was as much a formality as the arrest of the thieves themselves.

St Paul's Church and War Memorial

When the Napoleonic Wars ended the townspeople of a thriving Honiton decided to organise a carnival of celebrations. They invited people from all over East Devon to participate. Beer and Seaton sent a cart load of smugglers and Branscombe sent a donkey chaise full of lace makers. The best contribution came from Colyton where they harnessed the first ever wagon built in that town, a beautiful blue and scarlet contraption, and filled it with the local band. Hundreds of people descended on Honiton for a grand ball where the bandsmen of Colyton entertained. The beat to the music was tapped out in a highly original way by Sebastian Isaac, a trader who used his wooden leg to keep time and beat it with such enthusiasm that his peg almost fell off!

One of the more famous people to pass through the town was Horatio Nelson who spent a night at Honiton and performed a most noble deed. One of his best men, Captain Blagdon Westcott, had been killed in the Battle of the Nile. Nelson invited Westcott's mother and sister to have breakfast with him. On hearing that she had not received a gold service medal, to which her son would have been entitled, had he survived, he took a medal from his own coat and presented it to her.

It may be an old wives' tale but ... in Honiton's early days it was found that most of the women were barren. It was decreed that the good ladies had to visit St Margaret's Chapel where they must pray, but not 'just a quickie' – they had to get down on their knees for a whole day and night. Having done this a vision would appear to them thus making them pregnant...

We digress – our river has managed to bypass Honiton without being noticed. However the Otter has to be more wary of the potential predator that lies in wait just a few miles downstream.

Wolford Chapel – A Little Bit of Canada

The River Wolf is actually a lot tamer than it sounds! The small river of about three miles in length rises on the edge of the Blackdown Hills and flows down from the north to join the Otter on the outskirts of Honiton. Awliscombe, with a population of about 350, is about the only settlement of any size that it passes through but close to where it rises is a tiny bit of Canada! Wolford Chapel is the burial place of John Graves Simcoe (1752–1806) who was the first Lieutenant Governor of Upper Canada in the years 1792–96. Simcoe grew up in Exeter, was educated at Eton and Oxford and later had a long military career. In 1781 he married a lady of great wealth, Elizabeth Posthuma Gwillim, and bought a 5,000-acre estate near Honiton, which remained the family seat until 1923. However, he was an ambitious man and after a spell as MP for St Mawes in Cornwall, developed a wanderlust that was to see him on his travels yet again. He did a lot of work

for the British in Upper Canada and was a compassionate man of vision and energy. Much of the development of roads, and relations with native North Americans, was attributable to his efforts.

Wolford Chapel was designated as Ontario property in 1966 and there is a steady stream of Canadian visitors who probably feel a little less homesick on this small plot of land where their flag flutters proudly in the breeze.

Awliscombe has been interpreted as meaning 'the settlement in the forked valley', three streams uniting above the village. It is a place that I always seem to see in the dark for the only times I have stopped there have been to give talks to the WI. On one occasion, when they told me that they had a lot of business to discuss prior to my talk entitled 'Ghosts in Devon', I decided to pop in to the Awliscombe Inn, just yards away, to investigate another form of spirits. It was early evening when I strolled in but the suddenness of my entrance seriously startled the occupants ... they had been talking about ghosts and I had spooked them more than I did the WI some while later!

Buckerell

Buckerell, much closer to the Otter, is a small village but in relation to its size grew considerably in the years between 1971 and 1981. Its population shot up from 225 to a staggering 293, about a third more! Historians have championed the quality of some of the church's furniture. Within St Mary and St Giles is a monument to Samuel Graves, Admiral of the White, who lived at nearby Hembury Fort. He had the task of enforcing the Boston Port Act. This followed the Boston Tea Party when, as you may well remember from history lessons, trouble was 'brewing' when great amounts of tea were thrown into the harbour. The passing of the Act was seen to be one of the principal causes of the American War of Independence. The creator of the monument was John Bacon, RA who also has sculptures in Westminster Abbey and St Paul's Cathedral.

The village enjoys a lovely location with views across the Otter valley towards the towering heights of Gittisham Hill, which rises high to the south west of Honiton, on the south side of the Otter valley. The top of this hill is another plateau, this time with quite an extensive, but somewhat flat, uninteresting-to-the-eye, common spreading out over a great many hectares. Tucked into its north western flank is a picturesque village of thatched cottages.

Gittisham

Gittisham is located on yet another small tributary of the River Otter, the diminutive but charmingly named River Git! The village is famous for being the birthplace, in 1750, of a lady who attracted a lot of attention in her life and also afterwards! A simple country girl, Joanna Southcott caused a great deal of controversy by making all sorts of wild claims and prophecies. Without the aid of satellites she started by predicting the weather, moved on to forecasting political changes, but was more or less wrong, or well off the mark, with each prediction. Undaunted, she had them published and achieved fame and notoriety by challenging bishops to test her powers. She also sold 'Passports to Heaven', These ranged in price from 60p to £1.05 (a guinea). For a country person in eighteenth-century Devon this was a considerable amount but if it assured the possessor access through those Pearly Gates then it was surely money well spent.

At the age of 64 she announced that she was expecting a baby and that the child would be the next Messiah. Alas, the prediction was sadly awry for she wasn't with child, she was dying from dropsy (oedema). With this condition swelling of the abdomen occurs due to an abnormal accumulation of fluid in tissues of the body. Thousands of people had

Along The Otter

become her devout followers and there are still those, years later, who wait in great anticipation for the conditions to be right, when a sealed box of prophecies would be opened in the presence of 24 bishops. This, she maintained, would provide a panacea for all the ills of mankind.

Despite the dubious nature of her claims, she had many followers known as Southcottians, many of them from Sidmouth. The men were easily recognisable as they refrained from shaving and possessed very long beards.

These ardent followers fully expected her to rise again, within four days of her death, but she didn't return, presumably having used her own 'Passport to Heaven'. X-rays on her precious sealed box showed that it contained a pistol and other unidentified articles but no visible cure-all for the ills of the world.

Thomas Putt was an educated Gittisham man who became a barrister but his real legacy was an apple that he produced, called the Tom Putt, from which extremely fine cider can be made. He was regarded as something of an ill-tempered man so the drink might alternatively have been called 'Grumpy's Scrumpy'.

Fenny Bridges

The railway from Honiton to Exeter runs on raised ground above the flood plain of the River Otter to cross a battle site of the 1549 Prayer Book rebellion at Fenny Bridges. Here the rebellious Cornish found the government forces, led by Lord John Russell, rather too much for them. A tiny cross-swords symbol on the Ordnance Survey map does not reflect the great amount of blood that was shed, in the name of religion, on these green and pleasant meadows beside the Otter. According to the great folklore expert, the late Miss Theo Brown, "The country folk were armed only with billhooks and staves while the King's forces, besides being well armed, were assisted by foreign mercenaries who were astonished at the fight put up by our westcountrymen." It's said that, on a moonlight night, you can see ghostly horsemen plunging about the meadows, up to their hocks in blood.

The river has not always behaved itself in this vicinity, floods having wreaked havoc from time to time. It's believed that, in 1752, severe floods washed away St Anne's Chapel, which stood beside the Otter. Strangely, however, more than thirty-five years later it is mentioned in the parish accounts as being a 'Poor House'.

Feniton

The next station along this line is Feniton but rail enthusiasts will have fond memories of the days when it was 'Sidmouth Junction' and when the comprehensive railway network offered far more choice of destinations. From here, as the station's former name would imply, it was possible to catch the train to sedate Sidmouth. And as we will see

later it was also possible to travel along much of the lower Otter's valley to Budleigh Salterton and anon, inland to sunny Exmouth, Devon's driest place.

The main line to Exeter opened on 18 July 1860 revolutionising the pattern of trade and transport across the region, new horizons being opened up to places and areas that may have been previously regarded as backwaters. Feniton's station has greeted royal guests and a few celebrities. Do you remember the bouncing puppet known as Muffin the Mule? The good lady who was inseparable from this children's favourite of yesteryear was Anne Hogarth, a regular passenger here, when she lived at Whimple.

Feniton is a settlement of two distinct parts, the 'old bit' in and around the church and the newer part close to the railway station where a modern estate has mushroomed over the years. The population of Feniton in 1961 was a mere 320. Now it's more than five times that number. Not many of the 'newer' villagers will recall the problems faced by the villagers of Feniton in the early years of the twentieth century for they felt cheated that they, unlike most other old villages, didn't have a village green. What space they did have, at the cross-roads near the church, was used as a dumping ground by road builders who placed great mounds of chippings on the triangular space. But salvation was at hand and in May 1938 this item appeared in the local press to accompany this scene:

"Feniton today became the proud possessor of a Village Green. The tape that acted as a barrier was cut by Lord Sidmouth, and now the green is open to villagers and all-comers. The seat around the well-shaped tree will be a popular rendezvous." The Rev S. J. Ford is shown addressing the crowd.

Not too far from the river Otter's tinkling waters is a beautiful monument beside the busy A30, between Fairmile and Fenny Bridges, just three-quarters of a mile down the road from Feniton's station. A few passers-by are curious about its origin but most are completely blind to its existence even though they may regularly travel this important highway. One motorist, unfortunately, reduced it to a pile of rubble when in collision with it. But, like the Phoenix, it's risen from the ashes. It commemorates a remarkable man, Bishop Patteson.

On April 1, 1827, John Coleridge Patteson was born to distinguished parents and despite his birth date he was no fool! His father was Sir John Patteson and his mother a member of the Coleridge family, hence his middle name. He was a man of many attributes excelling at sports and also at languages for in his subsequent travels he picked up more than twenty. His father, a leading judge, bought Feniton Court when John was fourteen. He spent three years at the Foundation School at Ottery St Mary before going on to Eton.

At Oxford University he demonstrated his academic prowess, gained by hard work rather than by natural ability, by becoming a fellow of Merton. The next step was into the Church, with 'Coley', as he was fondly known by then, taking up holy orders in 1853. His first post was at Alfington, close to his home. However, it wasn't long before the green hills of his homeland were forsaken for the tropics. One of his father's friends, Bishop Selwyn, came to stay at Feniton Court and, in conversation, it was discovered that he was in the country trying to recruit workers for faraway places. Young John seized the opportunity and, as soon as arrangements could be made, he was off. His evangelical travels led him first, in 1856, to New Zealand and then to the South Seas and he so impressed the powers-that-be with his friendly willingness and pleasing ways that, by 1861, he became the Bishop of Melanesia. This was the same year as his father died at Feniton Court.

However, despite many exciting, but highly dangerous, episodes fate decreed the Bishop was not going to make old bones. His work took him to the island of Nukapu, his visit occurring just a short while after a band of unscrupulous English sailors had murdered five of the islanders whilst recruiting men for the slave trade. Unbeknown to the Bishop, his name had often been used to advantage by these men. Therefore, if you'll excuse the play on words, bearing in mind there were still many practising cannibals amongst the islanders, he wasn't exactly the flavour of the month! 'Coley's' timing couldn't have been more unfortunate for, instead of being afforded the customary hospitality, he was killed. He had stepped ashore, alone and unarmed, for he was a man

of peace who had befriended thousands of South Sea islanders in the many years he had been working in that part of the world. His body was placed in a canoe, bound up in native matting and, symbolically, was tied with five knots, each a symbol to represent the five islanders who had been murdered by the English a short time before.

Once the islanders realised their dreadful mistake, they were overcome with remorse and a cross was set up on the place where he was slain.

Queen Victoria was not amused for she referred to the Bishop's murder in her speech at the opening of Parliament. In addition to the monuments already mentioned in his memory, he is also recorded in the Gilbert Scott-designed 'Martyrs' Pulpit' of Mansfield stone, erected in 1877, at Exeter Cathedral. It has three panels to three martyrs, the other two being St Alban, who was beheaded and St Boniface, Crediton's hero, who was also slain. He is also remembered at Alfington's church of St James and St Anne where there is a marble monument to his memory. At the entrance to the church is a lych gate, which is a commemoration of Queen Victoria's Diamond Jubilee celebrated in 1897. It carries these inscriptions: "VR, 1837–1897" and "Alfington hereby commemorates the 60th year of Britain's Queen, Victoria the Good." It was the work of a local carpenter, William Basten, who used oak from the nearby Escot estate, and its lamp was bought from the Exeter firm of Wippell's. It was unveiled by Lady Kennaway.

Alfington is a small village and is occasionally inconvenienced by being mistaken for the phonetically similar Alphington of Exeter. It has also suffered from speeding traffic along its narrow, bendy lane.

Fairmile

The Bishop Patteson roadside monument stands on a low ridge of land between the Otter and one of its major tributaries, the Tale. This East Devon river rises in the hills, where the gliders gracefully float on the thermals, above the village of Broadhembury.

It flows to the west of Payhembury, giving it quite a wide berth, before missing Talaton by an equal distance to the east. The river influences such names as Talewater, Talaton and Taleford near Fairmile. The latter is a small hamlet with a pub, the Fairmile Inn, reputed to be a place where Oliver Cromwell personally killed a Royalist soldier and had another hanged from the rafters!

Escot, in the valley of the Tale, just to the north of Fairmile, a much more peaceful place, is now a tourist attraction with its aquatic attractions and fine gardens. A house has been sited here since 1227. The first truly grand house to be built here was by Sir Walter Yonge in the latter half of the seventeenth century. However, fate was not kind to it as it was destroyed on 28 December 1808. A post-Christmas dinner was brought to a sudden halt as a fire, started when curtains caught alight in an upper room, soon gutted the house. The uninsured owner lost a fortune in the flames whilst one worker, in trying to rescue people, was killed leaving a widow and six children. Although there was a large reservoir of water on the roof of the building, the speed of the fire prevented any way of using this to combat the conflagration. Nevertheless a large number of dinner guests filed safely out into the cold night air. John Henry Kennaway laid the foundation stone of the present house on 6 September 1837.

Just to the south of Fairmile, and after flowing under the route of the now disused Otter valley railway, the River Tale adds its waters to those of the Otter. This confluence is close to the architectural gem known as Cadhay House.

There's nothing like enterprise! John Haydon, a sixteenth-century man of influence and power, was an agent for Henry VIII, one of his jobs being to sell off the various religious buildings 'acquired' as a result of the Dissolution. It is just possible that, for an extremely modest outlay, he obtained much of the materials to build Cadhay from the demolished Dunkeswell Abbey, some ten miles away to the north-north-east. It's believed that he also negotiated the purchase of materials from the College of Priests from Ottery St Mary, just the other side of the Otter. With this collection of materials Cadhay House was built. Bearing in mind that the former abbey would have had a history, as indeed Cadhay House also enjoyed more than four centuries of occupation, it seems strange that it, apparently, has no ghosts of any note to walk its corridors.

The house is open to the public, at certain times, where guided tours of this lovely property will be a living history lesson. It is reputed that an apple tree in the grounds, of the Maid of Kent variety, is from a cutting, of a cutting, from the

tree that produced the historic apple that fell on Isaac Newton's head when he 'discovered' gravity. If you pay a visit, keep a look out for Edward VI, Mary, Henry VIII and Queen Elizabeth I. They are all there on stony, silent duty.

Ottery St Mary

But one of Devon's most attractive smaller towns waits for us beyond Cadhay Bridge. Ottery St Mary, which has in recent years, joyfully celebrated its 'Olde Ottery Week',

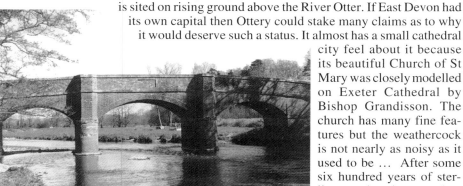

is sited on rising ground above the River Otter. If East Devon had its own capital then Ottery could stake many claims as to why it would deserve such a status. It almost has a small cathedral city feel about it because its beautiful Church of St Mary was closely modelled on Exeter Cathedral by Bishop Grandisson. The church has many fine features but the weathercock is not nearly as noisy as it used to be … After some six hundred years of sterling service, it was taken down for repairs in 1977. However, when duly repaired and replaced aloft, it gave out the most terrible piercing shriek, whistling down the wind, even in the lightest of breezes. The locals could not bear the sound so remedial work was done to ensure that the old weathercock, although still there, no longer crows or whistles over the close-knit rooftops of the town. It's believed that it might be the oldest weathercock still in use, dating back to 1342. What a lot of wind and rain it must have endured!

The church has had a great number of vicars in its long history, some extremely eccentric (as we have observed) and others so absent-minded that their antics defied belief. John Coleridge was such a man. Perhaps the production of thirteen children may have added to his total disarray and state of confusion. He was the classic example of somebody with an IQ as high as Mount Everest but one who lived completely in his own little world. He delivered sermons in Hebrew, to a congregation of Devonshire farmers and farm workers to whom the King's English would have been verbally challenging! When given a clean shirt to wear, by his second wife, he would put it on straight on top of the dirty one that he was already wearing. If this was not pointed out to him, he would continue to put on layer upon layer of shirts.

Despite this apparent 'eccentricity' his thirteenth child turned out to be one of our great poets, Samuel Taylor Coleridge, who was born here on 21 October 1772, at 11.00 a.m. Coleridge was one of the founders of the Romantic movement. In 1798 he collaborated with Wordsworth in *Lyrical Ballads*, which include *The Ancient Mariner*, and broke with the tradition of English poetry, writing *Kubla Khan* and *Christabel* at this time. Suffering from toothache, he took opium to alleviate the pain and soon became an addict, spending the last eighteen years of his life under medical care. But his memories from his Devon childhood remained with him. Perhaps he was thinking of the time when, as a child he had run away from home and fallen asleep, in the rain, on the banks of the Otter, when he wrote: *"Dear native Brook! wild streamlet of the West! How many various-fated years have past, What happy, and what mournful hours, since last I skimmed the smooth thin stone along thy breast, Numbering its light leaps!"*

It is said that when his father died, he went to his favourite spot, the Pixies Parlour or Cave, and cried bitterly.

Although most self-respecting pixies live on Dartmoor, or on its borders, there are pixies in East Devon as evidenced by the name of that cave, which is to the south of Ottery. The Rev. Sidney Cornish was another visitor to this cave and had this to say, in 1869, in a little book about the church and parish of Ottery St Mary: "The roots of the old trees form its ceiling; and on its side are innumerable cyphers, among which, the author discovered his own and those of his brothers, cut by the hand of childhood. To this place, the author, during the summer months of the year 1793, conducted a party of young ladies; one of whom, of stature elegantly small, and of complexion colourless yet clear, was proclaimed Faery Queen."

Pixies are mischievous characters and in 1454 they came out in great force to prevent the installation of the bell, to be known as St Mary. They first tried to prevent its casting, by withholding the necessary metals, but when that merely delayed the work, they rushed to the foundry at Exeter and dropped dew drops into the cooling casting. But the dew was so sweet with honey that the mixture improved the tone of the bell. Their last ploy to stop the bell reaching Ottery was to 'pixie-lead' the cavalcade to a steep cliff at Sidmouth but luckily one monk trod on a prickle and exclaimed "God bless my Soul and St Mary" and the pixies disappeared. They made one final gesture to prevent the bell being blessed, by binding the striking parts with magic cords. A special ceremony for breaking such an evil spell was conducted successfully. The pixies admitted defeat and agreed to leave the bells alone for 500 years. In 1954 Ottregian Fred Godfrey wrote *The Pixies Revenge* warning everyone to be on the lookout for the 'little folk' who might try to harm the bells now that their self-imposed half-millenium amnesty was over!

Having been scared witless once at Ottery St Mary myself, I have mixed feelings about an annual ceremony which is now synonymous with this East Devon town. Every year on November 5th the town is descended upon, from every direction, by many thousands of people who like a little 'spark of excitement' to light up their lives. Every available car parking space in and around the town is usually gone by early evening and the congregating masses line the narrow streets for the annual spectacle of tar barrel rolling.

The hollowed barrels have been coated many times with tar or bitumen over a period of months. Each of them is given the name of one of the pubs in the town and at the given time they are set ablaze and lifted aloft onto their bearers' shoulders. The nature of the game is to carry them along these streets, which are crowded with spectators, running in mazy fashion in and out of the spectators. The barrels burn for many hours and there are a large number of them so there is a sustained excitement about the ritual. The ceremony does not hark back to the Gunpowder Plot of 1605. It originated sometime towards the end of the eighteenth century. The participants protect themselves with layers of sacking, specially made gloves and stout clothing and apply a goodly amount of grease to any exposed skin in order to avoid scorching. The first burning barrels are relatively small but they get progressively bigger as the night advances. The pubs play an important role with most of them involved in the proceedings. They say, in Ottery, that the custom and practice of tar barrel rolling is not as dangerous as it appears but you need to know what you are doing! Vigorous attempts have been made to stop this event but nobody is obliged to attend and, after all, it is only one day a year. The pubs do a 'roaring' trade.

The tar-barrel rolling ceremony is just one item featured in the Ottery St Mary Hospital Embroidery. This splendid work of art was painstakingly put together by a large and enthusiastic team of stitchers led by Helen Bamber. In the period 1991–95 some two hundred people contributed to this masterpiece, which raised money for the town's new hospital. It is a massive work that shows many facets of life, and important buildings in the area that surrounds the town. Ottery's fine church, Bishop Patteson's Cross, Aylesbeare Common, Payhembury and the pixies, of course, are just some of the 50

stitched motifs. My favourite is the walker, to epitomise all the footpaths of the district, as it was designed from a picture of me! I had the immense privilege of applying the last of about 113,000 stitches at a ceremony at the Institute in early October 1995. If you visit the hospital, take a good look at the craftsmanship that went into the embroidery, which was created for everyone to enjoy.

Ottery St Mary has also inspired other writers than Coleridge. William Makepeace Thackeray spent some of his holidays here in the time about 1825–28, when he stayed at nearby Larkbeare, a mile or two to the north-west of Ottery, with his stepfather. In his book *Pendennis*, written 1848–50, Ottery becomes Clavering St Mary, whilst Exeter is Chatteris and Sidmouth is Baymouth. When another of his books, *Vanity Fair* (1847), was dramatised for television Sidmouth was used as the location. You can read more about that in my book about films and television programmes called *Made in Devon*. The River Otter has a far less attractive name as it was called the River Brawl in Thackeray's book.

In *Adventure Through Red Devon*, by Ray Cattell, he gave the Otter this passing mention, having seen it on a fine summer morning: "The Otter becomes a river of shining diamonds bouncing under the little bridges whilst the emerald meadows are incredibly rich with light." Anyone who has walked through the meadows beside the river will know exactly what he meant.

However there are those who wouldn't have seen the poetic loveliness of the valley for they were the hapless victims of the plane crash shown here, not far from the Salston Hotel, on land where Oliver Carter kept racehorses and where Point to Point races have

been staged. A group of passengers returning from Santander, on Thursday 17 July 1980, faced almost a catalogue of problems. They had been booked to get back to Devon by the car ferry that operates from this Spanish port to Plymouth, many choosing this mode of transport because of their fear of flying! But the ferry couldn't take them so as an alternative a flight was arranged to Exeter's airport. Alas, the plane, a Viscount 708, is believed to have run out of fuel; it had to crash land, its wing tip catching trees in the grounds of the Salston Hotel. Miraculously the plane spun to a halt in a field, at seventy acres the biggest for miles around, at Bishop's Court Farm beside the embankment of the former railway line beside the River Otter, killing four sheep as it did so. None of the other cows and horses in the field were hit but the animals panicked and stampeded, only being rounded up and calmed down some time later. Two lucky equine escapees were the racehorses 'Otterway', winner of the 1976 Whitbread Gold Cup and the champion horse, 'Ottery News'. The pilot was saddened by the death of the sheep as he was an animal lover. However he had done a marvellous job in landing the plane in such circumstances and the 58 passengers, none of whom came from Devon, and four crew, all survivors, were truly grateful. Those who had suffered cuts and bruises were taken to the Salston Hotel where the ballroom was adapted as a first aid centre.

Tipton St John

But all the while the River Otter, minding its own business, continues to meander peacefully through green and pleasant meadows towards, and then on past, the small village of Tipton St John (or Tipton St Johns), one which revels in the quiet life apart from the occasional footpath dispute or flood. Past experiences of the latter have taught the various hamlets and farms along the Otter to settle and develop, where possible, on ground above the level of the Otter's flood plain. The railway wisely ran on an elevated embankment for most of its way, al-

though in the floods of 1968 some wagons were marooned as the floodwaters left a section of line high and dry. The station at Tipton was an important one for it was here that the line split, one branch climbing the steep gradient of 1:45 to head on through Harpford Woods, under Bowd (meaning 'beneath the hill') and on to sunny Sidmouth, where the station was regarded as a 'fair step' from the sea front. It has been suggested that this siting of the station, some three quarters of a mile from it, was a deliberate policy to discourage hordes of daytrippers. Passengers on this railway would catch a glimpse of the yellow-bricked Harpford House, an unusual chateau-styled house where Lord Clinton lived, appropriately one of the directors of the London & South Western Railway. The line opened in 1874 but only survived until 1967. The through line continued on down the Otter valley. Tipton's claim to railway fame is that it was the last 'junction' station, between two single line branch lines, in the West Country, to close down.

The country around Tipton is glorious for walking although there have been problems with access at some points in the past. I have some painful memories of leading walks in this vicinity. Some years ago I was invited to lead the good ladies of Alphington Wives' group on a pleasant summer's evening stroll over the hills in this district. Last minute changes meant that my planned, and tested, route could not be done but as the 1:25 000 map showed clear public rights of way, from a point between Wiggaton and Tipton, over the hills into the valley of the Sid near Sidford, there seemed to be no problem. Not so! On your own you can 'make do and mend' but this was a nightmare, of the most public kind, and after battling with the Devonshire 'jungle' I would use the experience to warn others facing a similar adventure to be more thorough in their route planning and pre-walk preparations. Do not let your charges change the route at the last moment! There is often a disparity between what the maps consider to be walking freeways and what the impenetrable, barbed-wire, overgrown Devonshire jungle has to say about it all!

To the east of Tipton St John the steep scarp slopes rise, eventually, to Fire Beacon Hill. It's a demanding climb and those who braved it in the late 1930s had, according to the 1939 directory, the incentive of having refreshments at the Fire Beacon Tea Gardens provided by Mrs A. Baker, proprietress. The advert also claimed it to have 'the finest panorama of the West'.

Venn Ottery

Another small settlement to develop on the opposite side of the valley, on raised ground above the Otter's flood plain, is Venn Ottery. In the past it was also referred to as Fen Ottery, an indication that the surrounding lands were poorly drained. It's a quiet hamlet that has acquired several new homes in recent years, almost camouflaging its small church.

This small place lies in a depression formed by a tributary of the Otter that runs down from the heights of one of Woodbury's many commons. Although it's a peaceful place it was even quieter in those days before the motor car was given the freedom of the countryside. The hamlet had two larger farms, a small one and five cottages and a population of about fifty.

Nevertheless there were times when even this perfect peace was rudely shattered by a 'ghost'! The parishioners, who were more accustomed to 'living the everyday life of simple folk', were scared witless in the sanctuary of their own church.

The church is a modest edifice without the trappings enjoyed by larger ones. Within is a tablet to a man called Marshall Hare who died some centuries ago. The story goes that whenever the vicar, in the early 1900s, started to preach a sermon, loud tappings and rumblings would emanate from this commemorative stone. It was also reckoned that whenever these ghostly knockings occurred it would suddenly come over very dark. At such times the small congregation naturally became very frightened.

To rectify the problem a priest from Crediton was brought in to perform an exorcism. It's believed that at this service the spirit promised to leave the building and, apparently, agreed to be laid to rest in an area of wet ground some three quarters of a mile from the church. Another promise that was extracted from this spirit concerned the pace that it was allowed to maintain in its quest to return to its old haunting ground. This was negotiated to be at the rate of one cock-stride per year, the notion being that its return would be several lifetimes beyond those troubled by its presence and, as the spirit had an eternity to fill, what difference did a few centuries make to it anyway? One could say that a slow walk in the Otter valley was a fine bit of exercise even for a ghost.

Mr Welsman was the landlord of the Exeter Inn in those years that were either side of 1900. He was something of a local bard and having heard the story of Venn Ottery's ghost was moved to pen the story in verse. The *Express and Echo*, Exeter and East Devon's evening newspaper, published it first in 1908 and again in 1910. However, in 1930 there was a twist in this tale that explains part of the hauntings. A grave-digger at work preparing a plot, fell through the bottom of the grave that he was excavating only to find himself in a tunnel. It was high enough to walk along in a bent over posture. In one direction it led to a panelled wall beside a large fireplace in the farm where our friend, Marshall Hare had lived, and ultimately, died. In the other direction it led to the church and, yes, you've guessed it, to a point immediately behind the commemorative stone that was the source of all the problems. It appears that someone indulged in having a bit of fun with the clergy. Was it Marshall's spooky safari or just someone a little bit more alive with a wicked sense of humour?

Harpford

Harpford is small, but pretty, the church tower of St Gregory's being its most obvious landmark in the journey down this part of the valley. In the churchyard is a memorial to a famous former vicar, Augustus Montague Toplady. He was a hymn writer, probably best known for his 'Rock of Ages' written in 1775, who spent a short time here. His last years, from 1768, were spent at Broad-hembury, in a tributary valley of the Otter but, suffering from consumption, he moved to London where he died in 1778 at the relatively young age of just 38. The memorial was not put there until 1913 and stands on the shaft

of a much older medieval cross. It's believed that the inspiration for the hymn came from sheltering from a storm in the cleft of a rock. Some believe that this was in the woods at Harpford and others have suggested that it was in the Mendip Hills where there are many rocks and numerous clefts, of the limestone variety. Nevertheless Harpford Woods are wonderful, with their awesome oaks and beautiful beech trees, a perfect backcloth to a picnic in fine summer weather, people having enjoyed such alfresco meals here for generations. The only thing to disturb them in the past would have been trains on the branch line to Sidmouth that ran through the heart of Harpford Woods.

Newton Poppleford

For quite a large, or should we say long, village, nearby Newton Poppleford remains almost anonymous when it comes to featuring in books about Devon. Writers, since time immemorial, have glossed over it and one could, perhaps, draw the conclusion that it would, on face value, be the ideal place to live if you wanted to let the world go quietly by. The 1975 *Shell Guide to Devon* managed just eighteen words to sum up the village.

A lecturer of mine, from student days, was a well-known writer of many local books, S. H. Burton. He lavished just thirty words on Newton Poppleford. The late, eminent Professor W. G. Hoskins, who wrote the 600-plus page book *Devon*, had this as his total entry for the village: "Newton Poppleford stretched along the main Exeter–Sidmouth road, contains much decent building in cob and thatch. The church of St Luke was erected in 1897." But that was 26 words more than in Arthur Mee's 500-page *Devon*, first published in 1938, for that has no mention of Newton Poppleford at all! Even Eggesford with a population of just eighty, less than a tenth of Newton Poppleford's population, was included in his mammoth tome. So why has the village been neglected by writers? Is it really so dull and dreary? I don't think so!

Many people make pilgrimages to this Otter valley village, running at almost a right angle to the river, in search of the cream tea that is designed to defeat the appetite of most normal folk. They leave feeling a lot heavier than when they arrived and those foolish enough to make this a half way house whilst on a long walk find the rest of their safari hard going. The village might almost be regarded as the Cream Teas capital of Devon as there are so many places in and around the village where they may be enjoyed.

The name is one of the longest in Devon, many people simply referring to it as 'Newton Pop' for short. The 'popple' part of the place name refers to those beautifully rounded, smooth stones or 'popples' found in this part of the county, so often used in walls as an attractive ornamental feature. The original 'ford' or crossing place over the Otter is now usurped by a bridge. The village is one of the longest in Devon, in proportion to its population, even though it has grown slightly tubbier around its 'midriff' in recent years. It's also the one place on the road journey from Sidmouth to Exeter where there is almost bound to be some sort of obstruction to extend the journey time for travellers passing through. Whether it be roadworks, obstructive delivery vehicles or boulders falling off the back of Sidmouth-bound lorries there always seems to be something in the way. From the pedestrians' viewpoint there always seems to be a constant stream of traffic passing through and this has had its consequences with accidents and campaigns for better facilities for crossing the road.

If you have ever played 'Trivial Pursuits' you will, albeit unwittingly, have had a connection with this village for the brains behind many of those tip-of-the-tongue brain-teasers has lived in the village for some years and is 'Heighly' thought of by those who know him …

And if we're looking for trivial facts about Newton Poppleford we can start at the toll house, at the Exeter end of the village, because it is believed to be the oldest in Devon. It was built in 1758 when the traffic was decidedly quieter than these days. Another little gem of useless information is that Newton Poppleford gave the world the King Alfred daffodil. Gardener Harry Hill grew these fine blooms. Once bundled, they were placed on a cart and trundled down to Newton Poppleford's station from whence they were taken to London's Covent Garden. Sadly, the plot where this daffodil was first cultivated is now a modern housing development but at least it's named King Alfred Way.

The village once had two annual fairs incorporating an ancient tradition that wasn't always appreciated. Here is a letter that a famous Exeter-based church sculptor, Harry Hems, wrote to a local newspaper in October 1881 on this very matter. It appeared under the heading 'Horn Blowing'.

"Newton Poppleford is a Devonshire village upon the Otter, where much Honiton Lace is made. Its ancient parish church is dedicated to St Luke, and there are two annual fairs held, one upon Holy Thursday, and the other upon the first Wednesday after St Luke's Day (October 18). A very old custom exists at this place of blowing horns upon the Sunday night prior to the fair. The noise made thereby is as truly hideous as it is discordant. Thirty years ago steps were taken to put down the custom, which sober old stagers dubbed an unmitigated nuisance. The parish constables (no police existed then) took the matter in hand. So much feeling was produced by their interference that the noise became even greater than ever. Several of the ringleaders were summoned and had to pay rather dear for their pet hobby. But this did not deter them from carrying it on. However, when the spirit of defiance which had sprung up with the opposition to it began to cool, it was seen that horn would come to nothing. Within the last few years, instead of forty or fifty young men parading the streets on the Sunday night before the fair it has been left to a few boys, who disappeared when

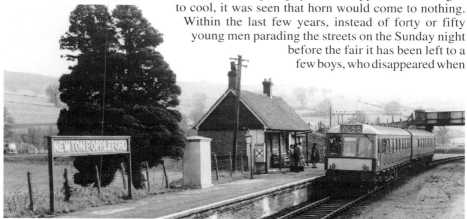

a policeman appeared in sight. The horns used for the occasion were bullocks' horns, and many of them have made close acquaintance with the heads of those who sought to silence them. There is one old horn in particular, now in possession of Mr J. Hans, which has been on active service for nearly a century, and its deep tone could be distinguished from all the rest even if fifty more were howling at the same time. It is said that the walls of Jericho fell down when the children blew their rams' horns. And well they might, no one would doubt it, if they ever heard horn blowing at Newton Poppleford.

"I have now to record that for the first time during the memory of living man the sound of no horn was heard in the village last Sunday night [October 16, 1881]. Will the custom become obsolete? If so, perhaps the good people of Newton Poppleford, whilst carefully eschewing the 'echoing horn', will still occasionally find some satisfaction in blowing their own trumpets!"

Newton Poppleford has a history of staging its own carnivals, the earliest ones going back to about the turn of the century when torchlight processions involved most of the villagers. The 1903 carnival is one that left its mark for a cottage caught fire and was destroyed. In those days the music was supplied by two brass bands, one of them coming from the village.

Some of the village's past industries only remain in the memories of the village's older residents. Millmoor Lane was originally known as Factory Lane and at one time it boasted a silk factory. Another past industry was the manufacture of gloves but nobody seems to have a hand in this trade any more!

Those who pass through the village may be curious about a red telephone box, complete with clockface, in the garden of a house as the road begins its long climb towards the common. This was the work of clockmaker Ken Woodley, who bought and restored the clock to working order. There seems to be a procession of passers-by who slow down or stop to see it. It's probably one of the most photographed landmarks in Devon. Ken maintains many church clocks in East Devon, the one at Ottery St Mary being just one.

Well that's a few words more than most authors have managed about this East Devon village, set in the heart of some glorious walking countryside where it's easy to escape the pace of modern life. The natural scheme of things lies down the Otter valley, the river getting stronger with the addition of each small tributary stream, several coming down from the steep hills on either side of the valley.

The public right of way down the western side of the Otter to Colaton Raleigh is a pleasant one with enough undulation to make it interesting, once the back gardens and hedges of outer Newton Poppleford are left behind.

There are no major settlements on the east bank between these two places, the twisty, also undulating lane leading down the east side of the flood plain is a relatively quiet one, but more enjoyable when experienced on foot with views across to the commons that stretch and join to make the area generally known, to laymen, as Woodbury Common. Many tracks lead off this lane, to the east, to ascend Mutter's Moor, more of which is featured in *Around and About Sidmouth,* the book that carries on where this one finishes.

Colaton Raleigh

We are now in 'Raleigh Country' and will get to his birth place in due course but here we'll jump the gun and have his baptism first! It's possible that the infant Raleigh was christened here at Colaton Raleigh in the chapel at Place Court. The use of the 'Raleigh' in the village's place name probably helps to differentiate the village from Colyton, farther east, to avoid confusion to the various postal and delivery services.

This small village is bisected by the A376 Budleigh–Newton Poppleford road, although the lion's share of the properties lie to the eastern side of the road. It has developed in the valley of a stream that rises a few miles to the west, close to Woodbury Castle. The Royal Marines will be very familiar with the marshy headwaters of this stream!

Although it's only academic now, the village didn't have its own railway station, even though it had its own

The only portrait published during Raleigh's lifetime – 1617

sidings. The nearest was East Budleigh, and that was literally a stone's throw, for someone with a good arm, from Otterton.

Colaton Raleigh's residents must be a determined bunch for they started their campaign for speed restriction signs limiting traffic to 30 m.p.h. in 1946. Some thirty years later, in 1976, they got their wish.

The village has had its share of characters. One of them was Granny Ebdon whose life ebbed away in November 1937. She had been a famous lace maker and her passing was so bemoaned that the church bell struck one ring for every year of her life, which must have been many for she was the oldest resident in Colaton Raleigh at that time.

Bicton

Bicton is now a well-known name because of the famous agricultural and horticultural college, established in 1957, where many students have received their first academic introduction to the more scientific side of a career in welly boots and Range Rovers.

Bicton House, former home of Lord Clinton, was built about 1730 but is not the first on the site as two previous mansions have existed here. The various families and personalities who have lived here through the centuries have been influential ones, shaping history far beyond the lands of the Otter valley. The great number of names of buildings and roads in East Devon's towns and villages is a reflection of this – Clinton, Rolle and Trefusis being just some of them.

However, visitors to the area are far more likely to visit the adjacent Bicton Gardens, a tourist attraction of great beauty, these being the landscaped grounds of Bicton House but almost divorced from the elevated red brick edifice by the lake. The miniature woodland railway, built in the early 1960s, at a time when the railway network, nationally, was reducing, skirts its south eastern rim. The railway builders managed to acquire signals, originally erected by the London & South Western railway, from Lympstone, on the Exe estuary.

There is much to see in these gardens, including tropical houses, exotic gardens, trees from all over the world, collections and to cater for children there are plenty of entertainments and activities. We have been brief here for this tourist attraction is well documented in its own literature and a visit will reveal all.

What the visitors won't see, nor most members of the public, is the China Tower that stands on private land in the woods at Baker's Brake, to the north-north-west of Bicton House. It was built as a most unusual birthday present, about 1840, for Lord Rolle who was on the mend after a long illness. His poor state of health was taken into consideration by the architect who designed a winding staircase wide enough for two of his minions to safely carry him up the 120 stairs to the top of the tower. The building got its nickname because Lady Rolle eventually used the tower to house her magnificent collection of chinaware that she had acquired from all corners of the world. Alas, the tower, part of which can sometimes be spied from the heights of Woodbury Common, possesses no such treasures today.

The Brick Cross or Bicton Cross stands at the cross-roads a short way down the road from Bicton. It has existed since 1743 and on each of its faces is a religious text, the north side perhaps being the most significant as it says, "Oh, hold Thou up our goings in Thy paths that our footsteps slip not." Three of the four texts include the word 'paths' whilst the fourth settles for 'ways', however mysterious may they be. It is rumoured that 'witches' were burnt at the stake near here in the past. Does a nearby disused chapel have something to do with this…?

– Plan –

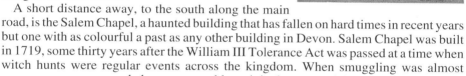

A short distance away, to the south along the main road, is the Salem Chapel, a haunted building that has fallen on hard times in recent years but one with as colourful a past as any other building in Devon. Salem Chapel was built in 1719, some thirty years after the William III Tolerance Act was passed at a time when witch hunts were regular events across the kingdom. When smuggling was almost regarded as a respectable activity by some of the locals, this chapel's roof, believed to be unique for it was an inverted roof forming a handy, out of eyesight, dip, complete with trap door, was used

to store contraband. Now it's well-known that smugglers would spin scary stories to frighten people away from their illicit booty but the chapel has had its spooks. The ghost of a lady, dressed in black, has been seen a number of times but the more common occurrence is the sound of children either laughing or crying, a reflection of some of the sadder moments from Salem's past.

The most amazing thing happened just after the end of a Sunday service. The chapel's electric organ, which had been used throughout the service, without problem, had been unplugged and covered over. However, with nobody sitting at it, or nearby, it suddenly started to play again, delivering a perfect rendition of a full verse from a hymn.

On a lighter note, the Minstrels' Gallery of the chapel may not have been the best place to have been in the past as it was held up, for some years, by a tree trunk. Congregations of yesteryear, apparently, were divided between the wealthier worshippers who sat on the downstairs level whilst the poorer parishioners sat upstairs, nearer Heaven!

Otterton

Otterton, just down the road from Brick Cross, is on the eastern side of the Otter valley and is snugly installed in its own valley of a small tributary stream that runs down beside the village street. It may look a tame affair but it's had its moments, flooding the village on a number of occasions. The Otterton Brook rises a few miles to the north east on that elevated ridge of land that has Mutter's Moor as its central portion. From these heights it falls first towards the coast but baulked by the high red cliffs of Windgate, it turns south-westwards through some of Devon's most fertile lands to make its way through Otterton and on to add its flow to that of its larger relation, the Otter.

Otterton features in another of my books *Around and About Sidmouth* so some of its more unusual stories have been left out of this book in order to avoid unnecessary duplication. Therefore this is just a brief mention of one of Devon's loveliest and most photographed villages.

It is probably this part of the valley which is most favoured by walkers as the green, flat and pleasant meadows between here and Budleigh Salterton are easy on both the eye and the feet. At weekends there is a continual conveyor belt of ramblers of all shapes, sizes and ages, most with a canine companion, following the Otter on its west bank. Those with a bit more adventure in their bones and enough puff to progress from the flats to the hills will inevitably do one of Devon's most walked triangles. Most walking guide books include this classic route that leads from Otterton to the coast at or near Ladram Bay. The route then heads south west along the low, but deeply red cliffs until the mouth of the Otter is reached at Otterton Point. The corner is turned, the route heading north to White Bridge, half a mile up river. Here the undulating path of the east bank gives way to the meadows of the west and the weary wayfarer wends his or her way back to Otterton. Of course it's possible to go the other way round or do an abridged version like the one in *Ten Family Walks in East Devon*. Wind direction and strength often dictate the way this tide of trekkers trudges but it's a good walk of variety although to the lover of hills, walking the flat section beside the Otter may be tedious.

Otterton Mill sees a lot of these wayfarers who take time out for a visit to the craft centre beside the Otter. The village green, complete with its Otter, is a most pleasant open space from which to begin a walking tour of this village, which has won 'Best Kept Village' awards. In summer the whole place is a riot of colour and well worth an hour of anybody's time for a brief browse around. There are those 'roses round the door' type cottages but nothing is overdone.

The church of St Michael sits on a high bluff above the river. It was largely rebuilt in 1871 and in doing so it was found necessary to do away with the vaults that stored the remains of the Duke family, large landowners in this area. It's highly likely that members of this celebrated family would have been given impressive funerals to send them off. However, when the church was rebuilt their skeletons were exhumed and unceremoniously dumped into a wheelbarrow to be carted off to a large trench where they were re-buried. This was supposedly done at night, almost in the fashion that suicides were

buried long ago. Death, particularly if it has occurred beyond the living memory of those charged with sorting the remains, thus appears to be a great social leveller, with no special treatment given to the rich and privileged. Otterton, although losing victims in the various plagues, was generally regarded as a place where you might expect to lead a long life for several persons have been known to make it through to the century mark.

However, if you have time on your hands you may care to lift your eyes aloft towards the church tower where a clock ticks the minutes slowly away below Otter valley skies. But it has a tale to tell… A well-known local miller, at the time when the church was being rebuilt, kindly donated the clock to the church. He thought it would be of personal use to him – whenever he wanted to know the time, all he would have to do is to look up. But life is never quite that simple – the clock was placed on the east side of the church tower, therefore only visible to everyone up the village's main street. Poor Miller Tetbury was not a happy man because he could not see his valuable gift from his place of work. Naturally he complained and the clock was then repositioned to face north instead, where it can still be seen to this day.

East Budleigh

Although our next featured village is East Budleigh, it has more than its fair share of Otterton connections. East Budleigh Market was held near the railway bridge here, and the station beside the Otter was, as we have already said, East Budleigh even though it was just the wrong side of the river from Otterton. The naming of some stations in Devon has caused confusion and there are many examples like it. The station in the centre of the village of Bickleigh was called Cadeleigh and the station at Exton was called Woodbury Road. Here, at Otterton, the problem could have been even more confusing for it was mooted that the station would be referred to as 'Budleigh Station' and the one at Budleigh Salterton would be 'Salterton Station.' This was because people always referred to the latter as 'Salterton' and the former as 'Budleigh'. So perhaps the final choice of East Budleigh was about right after all. Had the line been on the east side of the Otter, the station would have been Otterton and that would have simplified things.

In the railway's early days passengers waiting for trains coming down the valley from Tipton St John were given advance warning of the impending arrival of their train. The station master at Tipton St John had an extremely large bell that, given suitable weather conditions, could be heard on the village green at Otterton about four miles down the Otter valley.

Rivalry between Otterton and East Budleigh, two adjacent parishes divided by the Otter, has been quite fierce in the past and the river has played its part in settling some differences of opinion between rival factions. Rogation Day was chosen by villagers from East Budleigh as a day for beating the parish bounds, a perambulation that took them to their bank of the river Otter, but to a point farther downstream. Aware of this many villagers from Otterton would be there to give them a watery reception. The free-for-all usually ended up with more folk in the water than out of it.

East Budleigh is a beautiful village, a place where I have given a number of talks and have always been made extremely welcome. It's impossible to read anything about this village without finding a reference to the fact that Sir Walter Raleigh was born at Hayes Barton, about three-quarters of a mile along Hayes Lane, to the west of the village. The young Walter had a happy upbringing, so much so that much later in life he tried to buy Hayes Barton from the Duke family and must have been crestfallen at his offer being turned down. This large house is set in pleasant walking country with lots of quiet lanes leading towards the open commons. Some are included in *Ten Family Walks in East Devon*, so if you are in need of some gentle therapy…

The babbling Budleigh Brook burbles its way down from the heights of Bicton Common, through Yettington and on to East Budleigh where it becomes a real feature of the village, several homes having their own little bridge over it. In the summer it's a common sight to see people staying in the area get out of their cars to take photos of the picturesque cottages garlanded in flowers. Had they been in East Budleigh about a century or so ago they could have snapped away at Honiton Lace makers for there were believed to be 48 exponents of this craft living in the village in 1900.

One lively ceremony, connected with the village, has provided its youngsters with a tasty bun or two. 'Bun Day' is believed to date back to the landing of William of Orange, an event in history that took place at Brixham on 5 November 1688. An East Budleigh woman was so delighted at the news of the Dutch import that she gave money so that the children would be able to buy buns. What she started has gone on to become a tradition. In more recent years the buns have been wrapped in paper and thrown from the church tower, one by one, to the eagerly awaiting schoolchildren down below. Originally 'Farthing cakes' were baked for the occasion that, for many years, was celebrated on 4 November. However, late in the nineteenth century, the vicar decided to alter the date to 1 November, All Saints Day, the parish church's patronal festival. Until this time an amount of money was also set aside for the bell-ringers to have cakes.

Just to the south east is Otterton Park, complete with fine red brick gateposts but not much else it's thought. It is believed that a manor house was planned within this park but it didn't get beyond the foundation stage, even

though the property was put on the market, in 1780, complete with some 150 free-ranging deer. What we do know is that there was a golf course here for an early *Mate's Guide* says: "A golf club was established in Budleigh Salterton, in 1894, the links consisting of nine holes, being situated on the high land in Otterton Park, where a small but commodious Pavilion was erected, and to the present year it answers its purpose very well and was well patronised. It has now been given up…" The article goes on to mention the East Devon Club on West Cliff, high above Budleigh Salterton, that took its place.

The Otter, meanwhile, between Otterton and the sea is, for the most part, not a wide river, almost uniform in its width, at first, as it flows seawards. You would hardly suspect that the sea was so close. But this hasn't always been the case, there being much historic evidence to confirm that this was a deeper, longer estuary in the past, well able to accommodate the vessels of the day as they entered this haven to unload or collect their cargoes from various locations.

The Otter Estuary

A look at the map suggests the occasional clue for the hill, rising sharply above Otterton, is Anchoring Hill. The wide, low level nature of this part of the valley means that it wouldn't take much of a rise in water level to create the illusion of an estuary once more. Indeed there have been times when the conditions have contrived to flood these low-lying meadows.

So what has changed things then? All along our coasts, where there is a great interaction between the sea and the land, natural forces, of wind, wave and current have had their, sometimes wicked, way with the landscape. Occasionally this has been in a destructive manner just like the way that the sea removed much of Sidmouth's beach in recent years and also caused problems farther along the coast at Seaton. But at other times it has been a constructive force depositing sand, shingle or stones to form beaches, bars or other barriers. This is what has happened at the mouth of the Otter. We all know that the sea doesn't have any personal grievance against those who live along its shores or who depend upon it for their livelihood but it does seem that it can, indeed, be a cussed force always appearing to do the precise opposite of what people want. Imagine, then, the despair felt by those fifteenth and sixteenth century merchants who traded out of this small, but adequately deep, estuary in their small ships as the great shingle bar was thrown up across the mouth of the river. Efforts were made to rectify the situation but the hand of nature was far too forceful for the limited engineering skills and resources available to those who lived and worked there at that time. Without the strong tides to help flush the estuary, the build-up of sediment and silt was hastened. The inlet became shallower with each new season. However, it still retained its estuary-like appearance

for several centuries. The first Ordnance Survey map, published in 1809, shows the estuary extending right across the broad flood plain of today and up to about a mile inland to a point where Clamour Bridge is now located. One of the earlier spellings of this was Clammer Bridge, clam being a bridge made from a fallen tree or tree trunk.

After this time work continued to reclaim the land. We were at war with the French, officially this time, and large numbers of Napoleon's troops had been captured, many thousands being held at the war depot at Princetown on Dartmoor. However, as most were fit men, various energetic projects were found to occupy them. Here in the Otter estuary, troops in the custody of Lord Rolle of Bicton, were engaged in the task of building an embankment as part of the reclamation scheme. But not everyone approved of the, so called, 'improvements'. Some felt the haven was unsuitable for trading vessels and would be of more use as reclaimed land. Others felt differently.

A joint letter to the press, from a master mariner and rear admiral, regarding a survey of the estuary, published on 25 September 1858, had this to say on the matter: "James Webber, a fisherman, 80 years of age, voluntarily presented himself, and stated that he remembered the river from his boyhood, and at that time the mouth was so wide that vessels of sixty tons could work in; and that he, himself, was master of a vessel that traded in the harbour, and had often discharged his cargo as far up as the upper salmon pool, where there was twelve to fourteen feet of water, and fish in great abundance was caught there. That the harbour continued in this state until about fifty years ago, or in about 1810, when, for purpose of enclosing a piece of land, a bank was commenced to be made, and a very large quantity of tons of rock was taken away from the east side of the entrance; and, through depriving the river of this large surface of back water, and taking away the ground and rock on the east side, and thus allowing the water to escape in that direction, the entrance soon became blocked up, and gradually came into the state in which it now is. That he is certain the bank and enclosure are the cause of the harbour blocking up. As proof of this – in the year 1824, in the great gale, the sea broke through the dyke, and allowed the water to flow over the enclosed space, when the effect of the back water was

such that in about a fortnight the harbour was nearly as good as ever … This was corroborated by several old fishermen and other residents…"

Whatever the truth of the matter is, it is certain from this that both Otterton and East Budleigh would have had far more of a maritime feel in the past than they do today. Now there is that distinct air of them both being in the heart of the glorious East Devon countryside. But in every situation like this one person's loss is another's gain. In another letter to the press W. S. Andrews also appeared to be somewhat miffed by the reclamation scheme, accusing Lord Rolle of adding "a few paltry acres of land they do not want, for surely Providence has been bountiful enough to them in this respect, already possessing as they do one of the most fertile and beautiful valleys on earth. I have yet to see the future Lord Rolle's yacht all 'ataunt' in the harbour he will restore, eh! and his gunboat 'Sun' manned by his own tenantry to defend, if need be, the bountiful possessions Providence has been pleased to bestow upon him."

Whatever the politics, sour grapes, or the arguments, to stand on the top of the great pebble beach at the mouth of the Otter, and gaze along the red Devon coast towards the south west, is a lovely, serene experience, particularly at sunset. Budleigh's beach was a busy place in the past with the arrival of paddle steamers, like the *Duke* and *Duchess of Devonshire*, and with the small fishing fleet which operated from here. There were also various imports. Until 1885 lime was brought ashore here in an unusual way.

Vessels bringing the stone from Brixham would arrive at the highest state of the tide. When as close in as they dare get they would unload the lime overboard into the sea. The tide would then retreat and those charged with the task would then load the stone into wagons on a tramway that led to the limekilns nearby. However, the method wasn't foolproof and there were many occasions when boats had to wait days before being able to off-load their cargo. Coal was delivered in the same fashion. After the closure of the kilns the coal was delivered ashore by flat-bottomed boats, called lighters. This trade also died out, about ten years later in 1895.

The lime burning was not without incident for in 1809 a man of 'reduced circumstances' took shelter there as it was warm. Alas, the kilns were lit and it was only after he had been cremated that anyone was aware of his charred presence.

One of the strangest invasions, apart from the more recent army of retired military men and their wives, to Salterton, was in 1901 when a school of octopi drifted in and around the rocks by the mouth of the Otter. Countless thousands of octopi drifted in to the shore and played havoc with the various crab and lobster pots. According-ing to those who witnessed this amazing spectacle, the lobsters and crabs, which had the misfortune to be caught in the pots, were sucked dry by the thousands of octopi dining out at the mouth of the Otter.

And now we must disentangle ourselves from this curious episode for our journey along this magical East Devon river has now run its course. We have engaged Jane's Fighting Ships, been on the trail of some Honiton hoodlums of yesteryear, been sidetracked by the railways, dodged the flaming tar barrels, met the 'Mystic Meg' of the eighteenth century, gazed at ghosts, met mischievous pixies, and all this in so short a time. Nevertheless the quiet riverside meadows remain a quiet and pleasant place to retreat to when the need arises. Perhaps if you now go and explore this lovely river for yourself, with fresh eyes, you may find your very own 'Passport to Heaven'! I hope you enjoyed this little journey 'Along the Otter'.

x Churchinford

Upottery x

Combe Raleigh x

x Awliscombe

x Monkton

x Buckerell

Feniton x

x **Honiton**

Fairmile x

x Gittisham

x Alfington

x**Ottery St Mary**

Venn Ottery x

x Tipton St John

Newton Poppleford x

x**Sidmouth**

Colaton Raleigh x

Otterton x

x Ladram Bay

East Budleigh x

Budleigh Salterton x

(not to scale)